55 Keys

Tips, Tricks & Tidbits for
Living a Happy & Successful Life

Alana Fairchild

BLUE ANGEL®
PUBLISHING

55 Keys

Published by Blue Angel Publishing
80 Glen Tower Drive, Glen Waverley,
Victoria, Australia 3150
E-mail: info@blueangelonline.com
Website: www.blueangelonline.com

Edited by Jeanette Hartnack

Blue Angel is a registered trademark of Blue Angel Gallery Pty. Ltd.

ISBN: 978-1-922161-54-3

Preface

YOU CAN LIVE A HAPPIER LIFE, a life of fulfilment and peace, where you feel good about yourself and experience success in a meaningful way. Living that life starts with listening to your heart.

Your heart is smart. When you wonder if there is more to life, or if there is an answer to a problem you can't seem to solve, your heart has the answers you seek. If you trust your heart, it will guide you through even the biggest challenges in life. Trusting your heart means you act on what you feel. Sometimes that means learning to live a different way, or doing something that may not seem to make a lot of sense but somehow *just feels right* anyway.

Trusting your heart to guide you, instead of just your head, will lead you out of doubt, depression, fear or boredom into a life that feels happier, more passionate, creative, inspired and successful.

It can be tricky to learn a new way to live, especially if you have been taught to toe the line, believe in logic instead of intuition and only believe in the things your family, friends or colleagues believe. You'll find your heart can help you though, giving you courage and a willingness to shake things up whilst still feeling safe within, as you create a better life for yourself. You may even end up inspiring your loved ones to do the same for themselves!

As you learn to listen to your heart, your inner world will change. You'll like yourself more. You'll feel more happiness and contentment. It will show. People will notice the difference. It may make them wonder what you've been up to (and if they can do the same!). Without saying a word, you'll come across as more confident and at peace with yourself.

Your life will start to look different too. It might begin with small changes, but when you really listen to your heart, there is no limit to the healing changes that can happen in your life. You'll feel as though you are living *the right life for you*, with success and happiness, and with things falling into place as though they are just meant to be.

HOW TO WORK WITH THIS BOOK

You can read this book through, perhaps one key per day, to help you connect with your inner wisdom to live with more happiness, courage and peace. Or you can treat it like a conversation with your own heart. You ask a question, become quiet, place one hand on the book and say quietly, "I call upon my wise and guiding heart. Please show me what I most need to know at this moment." Then open a page randomly. That is the message from your heart, and your key to happiness.

What the message is telling you might seem obvious, or you may need to 'read between the lines' and let the answer sink in over a day or two. There is no such thing as 'getting a wrong message'. You will always get the message you most need at the time.

1.
When Was The Last Time You Played?

FUN IS A NEED. I learned that from my fluffy orange cat. He would make a distinctive meow that wouldn't stop even when he had food, clean litter, an open door, a yard to explore, clean water and comfortable bedding. That particular meow only stopped when I paid him attention and entertained him. If I forgot to play with him, he became cranky and eventually depressed and withdrawn.

Human beings tend to go down the same route when denied their need for fun.Fortunately for my furry companion, it didn't take me long to work out what he was teaching me. Learning that lesson improved his quality of life – and my own – considerably.

2.

Letting Go

LETTING GO OF A PROBLEM is the fastest and easiest way to resolve it. Letting go doesn't mean pretending there isn't an issue or refusing to take action. It means giving up your worry or doubt and relaxing with a trusting attitude that it will work out somehow. The more relaxed you are the easier it is for the universe to step in and sort it out.

Have you ever tried to play with a dog that wants to run and chase a ball, but you can't throw the ball because he won't stop chewing on it? Until he lets go, you can't do your part so he gets what he wants! Human beings can learn something from that dog. The universe wants to help us, but we have to be willing to let go!

An easy way to let go is to ask or pray for help. Prayer can be powerful in ways the logical mind simply cannot understand. It just works. You don't have to be religious to pray. You don't even have to be particularly spiritual. You just need to believe in the possible existence of a greater intelligence or higher power. But if you aren't sure, you can pray anyway – treat it as an experiment! It doesn't really matter to whom or what you pray – God, Mother Nature or the universe perhaps. What matters most is *how* you pray. It's best with simple words with the expectation they are being received (somewhere, somehow), and that you will be helped in the best possible way with no expectation as to how that will happen. Having no expectation as to what the solution will be is important. Answers to prayers can be very quick. So don't focus on getting your answer some time in the future and miss the answer that ends up right under your nose!

A great prayer that anyone can say is: "I call on unconditional love to help me now with… *(whatever issue you need help with)*. Please guide me to the best solution. Thank you."

3.

One Size Doesn't Fit All

THERE'S NO ONE-SIZE-FITS-ALL APPROACH TO ANYTHING, especially health. A new trend is always just around the corner, soon to be followed by research that contradicts it. One thing I learned in law school (and managed to remember after I graduated) was that it is entirely possible to convincingly argue for one point of view before immediately, and just as convincingly, arguing for the entirely opposite point of view! I was promptly cured of any belief in a point of view being 'right' or 'wrong'. So, whilst I was open to learning from others, I avoided treating anything that was given to me as gospel. Instead, I experimented with what I learned until I found what worked for me.

There's a saying I have found to be true: one man's meat is another man's poison. What nourishes another may be downright destructive for you. There is no 'one right lifestyle' or 'one right diet' or even 'one right religion' that is going to bring happiness, health and inner peace to every body. We all have to find our own way, a way to live that will suit our temperament, constitution and our current phase of life. If someone tells you that you must live a particular way, then that is more likely to be about their own fanaticism than what is best for you. Recently, an acquaintance of mine said to another, "You are so extreme. It's good you are only interested in food and not politics because, otherwise, you'd be a terrorist!" Indeed!

So if there's no *one right way* to do anything, how can you find the best way for you? Listen to yourself and be willing to experiment. Try different ideas. Give yourself time to feel the results of certain choices; and once you find something that feels right, don't be afraid to change it again when it doesn't feel so right anymore. What works for you is likely to change as you do. Don't wait for the perfect solution that ends all your problems; instead, experiment with what works best right now.

4.

Closing Doors

A CLOSED DOOR IS A SIGN. You might think it is a sign saying no, but it's not. What it means is there is another way, a better way, a different way, to get to where you want to be. If you forget this and focus just on that closed door you can't seem to open, you could waste precious time and energy trying to force something, fighting against what is actually trying to help you. It's smarter to trust in the doors that close just as much as the doors that open. A closed door is just helping you move closer to the right door, the one that *will* open.

5.

Becoming Your Own Role Model

IF YOU WANT TO GROW UP rather than just get older, you'll need to become your own role model. It's great to be inspired by others; but whilst imitation may be the sincerest form of flattery, you were born to be YOU, an original, not a copy of someone else. When growing into the best version of you, there will be times when you really have no clue about who you are or where you are going. It might feel like an identity crisis or a painful sense of not knowing what you are doing in life, but these experiences are actually positive signs. You are choosing to not allow others to tell you who you are or who you should be; you are carving your own path in life.

You are brave enough to find your own way through life. At various times, you'll look back and be amazed at how you just kept going when sometimes it was really hard to not give up. You'll be so proud of yourself. You will become a role model for yourself and inspire others to take their own journey too.

6.

From Little Things, Big Things Grow

BIG HAPPINESS can come from small changes in your life. Making one small change that makes you feel good can boost your self-esteem tremendously and give you confidence to trust yourself enough to take bigger steps towards even bigger changes. However, trying to make lots of changes all at once is not such a good idea. (Am I the only one who dreams of complete transformation in only one week? I think not!).

For change that actually lasts (more than two weeks) it's better to take smaller steps that add up over time. You make progress every time you choose to live positively in the 'now', rather than waiting, worrying that it might not be a 'big enough' change or fretting over what you have or have not done in the past. So dream your big dreams, but don't underestimate the incredible power of the small gesture. Some small but significant steps you can take include: a walk in the afternoon; spending time in nature; turning off the TV to read or talk; studying, even just a chapter's worth; writing another page of your manuscript or journal; lighting a candle and relaxing for a few minutes before sleep; taking a proper lunch break instead of trying to 'work through'; expanding your social network or life experience by meeting new people or trying a new activity, even when that means putting yourself in situations where you may not be completely comfortable; attending a class to learn a new skill; buying organically grown and free range produce; drinking filtered water; or taking an afternoon nap. Small steps toward change on a regular basis soon add up to having travelled a long distance towards greater happiness and a better life.

7.

What You Speak About, You Bring About

YOUR WORDS HAVE POWER. In many cultures, words are used for both curses and blessings. Words have an effect. If you say something long enough, you'll start to believe it. If you keep saying it, you'll start to see it in your world. It's all because the power of your words has an impact on your life and the lives of others. Positive words, said with positive feeling, are like casting a spell (in a good way) for what you want. Negative words, said with intensity, can create consequences we really don't want. When you put out negative energy, you attract it back to you. Like attracts like. So when you put out positive energy, you attract more of that into your life.

If you are surrounded by people who think and speak negatively about themselves, about others, about life, try a little positivity. Add it into the conversation. Or consider spending some time with people who lift rather than drag you down! Remember to use words and expressions that match what you want to experience in life. You don't have to lie or pretend something isn't difficult when it is, but put a positive spin on it. You can meet a challenge and say, "Nothing good ever happens to me!" Or you can meet that same challenge and say, "I am strong enough to conquer this, and I am so proud of myself for taking up the challenge!"

Say what you want to experience. Tell yourself you are worthy, you are doing well and expecting good things in your life. If you catch yourself saying something negative, just stop for a moment, change the words and turn it into a positive.

What you speak about, you bring about. You are creating your life with every word you say. Even if you only repeat the words in your mind, the universe is always listening.

8.

Learning To Like Surprise Parties

LIFE IS UNPREDICTABLE. Even when you think it's inevitable that things are going to happen a certain way, there'll always be at least one twist you didn't see coming. This can be unsettling, but ultimately it's good. If life always performed according to our expectations we would miss out on so much.

When you realise you can't control life, you might feel afraid and become anxious or angry. But you can heal your fear by having faith. Faith isn't about religion; it is about finding inner peace amidst all the uncertainty of life. Faith is belief in something beyond what we can immediately see or understand. It's about trusting when there doesn't seem to be a reason to trust.

It's been my experience that although life has rarely matched my plans, it has helped me in so many ways with kindness, love and a sense of humour. My job is to listen to my heart and do my part, and when I've done what I can do (which is a lot, but also so much less than my once controlling mind used to believe), I let go and allow life to do the rest. Every unexpected alternative path life has presented to me has, without exception, been superior to what I had imagined for myself. It's had far greater and more positive repercussions in my life and what I bring to the world than I could have dreamed up, even on my best days. It's not any different for you.

Do what you can – knowing that this never includes controlling the world around you or the people in it – and have faith. Life has some amazing and beautiful surprises in store for you, most of which you won't see coming. That can make it all the sweeter – sort of like a surprise party.

9.
Trust Yourself

OFTEN, THE MOST DIFFICULT PART of making a choice is not the actual decision itself, the truth of which you probably already feel in your heart, but about trusting yourself. You might think you need to learn how to hear your intuition, though it's more likely you are already far more intuitive than you realise.

I have usually felt the inner urging of my intuition as a knowing or feeling in my heart, but what I have had to learn is to stop ignoring that intuition and act on it instead. Sometimes I would sense something about a person that wasn't nice. I would think it a terrible thing to feel that about someone, and so ignore it. However, I came to realise that ignoring intuitive insight is actually quite stupid. Painful circumstances I came to experience could have been avoided if I had listened to my intuition in the first place.

So I stopped doing that. I starting trusting my intuition instead, and when I did that my life completely changed. Trusting my intuition has helped me out of unfair financial and work situations, and has disentangled me from toxic relationships. It has easily found me lovely places to live, and has helped me diagnose my health issues. It has given me ways to earn an income and, of course, has provided me with excellent parking spaces!

Intuition will sometimes tell us things we'd rather not hear. I have learned that this is so we don't have to experience something we'd rather not later on! If you don't want to always refer to your intuition as 'that voice I wish I had listened to', then it's better to pay attention and give your intuition the benefit of the doubt, so it can become 'that voice I'm so glad I listened to'.

10.

Do You Dare?

YOU CAN TRY TO CONTROL LIFE (you'll lose that battle, by the way); or, you can choose to live like you are dancing with life, surfing its waves, caught up in its rhythms like a musician surrendered into the bliss of music.

People who choose aliveness instead of control are more fun to be around. It's like their inner light has been switched on. They have vibrancy; they often have no idea where they are going, but they always seem to be going somewhere interesting and good! They are willing to grow. They take risks that feel right – risks in work, risks in love, risks in life. Their optimism tends to be contagious.

People who are really alive are like butterflies. They have gone through struggles – sometimes very painful ones – and they have survived. They are beautiful because they still dare to dream, hope and love. People can feel optimistic, positive and uplifted just being near them. When something happens, these people choose how they want to respond rather than trying to force it to be different.

We try to control life to avoid pain, but that kills off pleasure, freedom and fun. It causes *more* pain and denies us the joys of life. I have never heard anyone who has chosen to let go of control and live more fearlessly say, "I miss my old controlling life." Not once. Not ever.

11.

The Only Rule Is There Are No Rules

THERE ARE NO RULES WE HAVE TO FOLLOW, not really. People who tell you that you have to follow rules are usually frightened. They build rules, like walls, to try to protect themselves from the uncertainties of life.

Rules are not truths. If you feel the need to hold on to certain rules of your culture, upbringing or religion, then understand that this is a choice you are making. If it feels like you don't have a choice, you are, out of fear, following rules made by others rather than figuring out what has genuine meaning for your heart. You can't be your own person if you are too busy trying to be who you should be, according to everyone else.

To find what you really believe in requires that you question what you've been conditioned to believe about yourself and life. You can feel a bit crazy when you challenge the things everyone else says you should just accept. But people who aren't afraid to break rules, and don't just accept whatever they are told, are typically found rocking boats and navigating them into new waters, rather than rowing around in circles not getting anywhere.

12.

What Do You Want To Believe?

YOU GET TO CHOOSE YOUR BELIEFS about everything. No topic is off limits, and you are always allowed to change your mind. You might think this is scary; I find it liberating. You might believe in fear and struggle, but you may want to believe in trust, flow and abundance.

The problem for many a dissatisfied person is their beliefs are not generous or loving enough to support their dreams and how they would like to live. They believe in fearful attitudes that keep them small when they want to live in a way that is fearless and bold.

If your beliefs are holding you back from the kind of life you want to live, it's within your power to change them. It can take courage and patience, but with both of those qualities, you will be able to do it. Just start thinking in that new way; and even if at first you feel you are being tested by life, don't give in! Let nothing divert you from it. Change the way you look at what is happening to reinforce the belief you want to have instead.

If you get used to changing your attitude rather than life, then life will respond to your new beliefs. You can look at the rain and see it as good for the garden or as a blight on your plans for the beach. It's still just rain, no matter how you view it. That one situation could have you believing: *Mother Earth is caring for life and I am included in that – I feel very grateful! Or, I never get what I want – typical that it is raining on my day off. I feel angry and miserable!* Whatever you choose to believe will create an attitude, an emotional response, an action, and either an increase or a decrease in your overall sense of wellbeing and energy. And all from what you choose to believe about the weather!

So whilst we cannot control life – sometimes it is going to rain whether we want it to or not – we can choose our beliefs and learn the art of taking life's lemons and turning them into lemonade.

When you look for the good in all things, the good in all things looks for you. Upgrading our beliefs to be more loving and positive is not about denying life's challenges. It's just about seeing them in terms of what they will give us, feeling proud of how we are handling something, and choosing not to give up because it will all be worthwhile in the end.

Realising that absolutely anything can be questioned, challenged and reflected upon gives us permission to tap into our power to choose our beliefs and feel more empowered. That permission can be enough to transform a life so dramatically that you will seem to become a whole other person. Yet on the inside, it will just feel like you are being yourself, more so, and with more happiness and inner peace than ever before.

13.

Your In-Built Timer Is Ticking

WE ALL HAVE AN IN-BUILT TIMER set for when we are meant to shine. It's a bit like an oven timer. You need to prepare all the food before you get it in the oven. If you didn't do that, the timer would go off with no meal cooked! However, after you prepare the food and shut that oven door to let things cook, it will all come together at the right time. You cannot make the oven cook any faster though. If you were to try to speed up the cooking process, you'd just end up with a burnt, dried out meal.

Being instilled with an at times impatient nature in combination with a slow-cooking pace of life has made me realise there's no way to change this, no matter how many times or ways you try. Some people just need more time to grow into themselves and find their place in the world. It's not a question of whether you are working hard enough or smart enough, it's just part of how you are built.

Late bloomers typically have depth in what they finally become able to offer the world because, just like a slow-cooked meal, their various ingredients have had time to blend and create a rich, nourishing flavoursome result. Early-blooming people can be more like a delicious and nutritious salad, but that is not always substantial enough when there is a greater need for nourishment.

So if you are a late bloomer, not quite having found your place in the world as yet, don't judge yourself. It's likely you are capable of a richer contribution to the world, but are blessed with a capacity for endurance and an ability to live with depth, which creates wisdom.

The 'meal' you eventually become to feed the world will be one to truly satisfy the hunger of human souls. You are just developing your capacity for such an offering, and so your in-built timer has been set accordingly. Just keep living your life and know that, in due course, the timer will ring. Your time will come, and you'll be utterly delicious!

14.

Age Is An Attitude

I BEGAN WONDERING if 'age appropriateness' existed anymore when I noticed grandmothers of sixty shopping with granddaughters of sixteen in the same stores for the same clothes. The rules about age are changing and we are the ones creating that change by choosing to exercise our freedom of choice.

You don't have to be a certain age if you want to get married or start a family, if that is what you choose. You could reach the peak of success in your career when you are thirty or when you are eighty. You are never too old to fall in love, to discover great passion, to learn something new, to start afresh after a challenging time or to feel like your life is an adventure.

If you are about to reach (according to your beliefs) a milestone age and are panicking because you haven't achieved something you think you are supposed to have achieved by now, forget about it. Rules about age only exist in your mind. You can feel confident and trusting in your own journey, and believe it is happening at exactly the best pace for you.

As you stop measuring yourself against an age-appropriateness rulebook you'll lessen anxiety and increase inner peace. Unintentionally, you could also become an inspiration for others. You can still be a successful, happy and vibrant person, even when (or especially when) you don't fit in with old-fashioned stereotypes for your age group.

15.

Money & Happiness

MONEY DOES NOT GUARANTEE HAPPINESS. Financial security can make the uncertainties of life seem more manageable, but there are plenty of people who are financially secure and very unhappy with their lives. I've experienced various financial states from windfalls to times where I had about twenty cents in my bank account.

My feeling of safety used to depend on how much money I had at the time. When I abruptly left regular employment and began working full-time as a spiritual healer, I felt relieved and happier on one hand, and yet there was so much unpredictability about my income that I also felt very anxious about how I was going to survive.

Nearly two decades later, I am happy to report that I did manage to survive and my deepest fears proved themselves to be nothing more than a product of a mind freaking out instead of trusting. The journey from freaking out to trusting wasn't easy however. I had to keep building a belief that I was loved and held by life and that it wasn't insane, irresponsible or childish to put some faith in my ability to relax and attract what I needed when I needed it. I worked hard but I handed over my sense of control regarding the outcome of all my efforts to the universe.

It took just over a year of intense daily emotional episodes of fear, panic and anxiety, each one typically lasting several hours, before I decided I probably wouldn't end up destitute after all. By about six months after that the panic attacks subsided. It was a long battle between fear and trust.

Eventually, I decided that if I chose to relax more, my financial as well as emotional wellbeing would likely improve. And that is what happened. Sometimes life went in directions where it was very easy to trust, and at other times it felt harder. I decided to treat the times during which it was harder to trust as opportunities to become more unconditional in my surrender to life. The more I trusted, the more my life unfolded with my needs being met, often in unexpected, gracious and sometimes quite humorous ways.

16.

Don't Chase The Good Stuff Away

IF YOU WANT TO ATTRACT MORE of something into your life, chasing it will generally have the opposite effect.

In my younger years, I believed that to attain a goal, I should go after it without restraint. I was successful many times with that approach, but not always. And it was always hard work. Not the sort of hard work that energises you and leaves you feeling inspired; it drained me completely and left me feeling depressed, even if I was succeeding. I would be too exhausted to be in the mood to feel good and celebrate!

There is another way to get to the good stuff in life. This other way is about inviting and receiving goodness into your life with less striving and effort. Think about it like this: two people are in a social setting and one is anxious and agitated, maybe looks polished but gives off a desperate vibe of need; the other looks relaxed, maybe a bit scruffy around the edges but feels good about themselves and is open rather than needy. Can you sense the attractive and magnetic quality of the second person that the first person lacks? It will not just be people drawn to that second person, but also opportunities and good fortune.

So how do we find that effortless way to attract what we want and need into our lives? Relaxation is the key. It is based on inner peace. Peace is not laziness or inactivity. Peace is being active in an effortless way. It is magnetic. It has its own pulling power. We don't have to go after what we want; it comes to us naturally, as if on a wave heading towards our personal shoreline. We all have peace inside ourselves. With some practice, we can learn to dip into that internal river of peace when we need it – even if things seem chaotic on the surface of our lives, or in our minds!

To generate that magnetic peaceful quality, find out what helps you relax. It could be meditation, dance, music, yoga. It could be swimming, nature walks or playing with a pet. Perhaps reading, writing poetry, painting, cooking, or even cleaning! Lying on your back and watching the clouds pass by, getting a massage, or learning to cultivate some reassuring and kind 'inner talk' and practising it regularly are some other examples.

Learning to relax helps teach your body and mind to go diving into that internal river of peace, and emerge with enough pulling power to keep your life filled with good things for which you can be grateful.

17.

Asking For Help

FIND A PRAYER, mantra or affirmation that appeals to you and use it often. The universe has a loving and benevolent streak, and if you ask for help, it will be given. It really does not matter exactly what words you use, what your religious path is or how spiritual you think you are. What matters is that however you choose to say your prayers, or whatever affirmation or mantra you choose, it feels right for you. You can even choose prayers from various religious and spiritual traditions, whether you personally 'belong' to that tradition or not. The universe won't mind at all, and anyone who tells you otherwise is speaking through fear rather than truth.

A simple prayer for daily use is: "Universe, please help me resolve all issues in my life quickly and with grace, mercy and kindness. Thank you!"

When you use prayer or affirmations daily – whether for a few seconds upon waking in the morning and before sleep at night, or in a more contemplative way, perhaps in conjunction with a meditation practice – you are creating your own personal spiritual practice. A spiritual practice will have a noticeable and positive effect on your life. It creates an internal sanctuary that helps you remain strong and centred when facing life's challenges. Instead of getting caught up in fear when life inevitably deviates from your plans, or when something shocking happens in the world and triggers panic in others, you will still feel steady and reassured that, in some way, life is working out the way it is supposed to.

18.

The Power Of The Human Heart

THE HUMAN HEART has powerful healing intelligence. It can go through pain and become more open, more loving, because of the experience.

I've seen people recover from disturbingly traumatic experiences. Rather than avoiding the pain and shutting down, they chose to face it and move through it. They used therapy and whatever help their family and friends could give and they didn't try to hide from what had happened. Eventually, they were naturally able to forgive things that many would think impossible. They chose to do it to make themselves emotionally free to live and love with hope for a brighter future. The past came to have no hold over them and they were able to live as loving and gentle people, without fear or bitterness in their hearts.

It takes courage to allow the heart to heal. It often doesn't feel good when you are healing as it often involves coming face to face with feelings you would much rather avoid. You have to trust there will be a point at which it will be over and you will finally be free. Trying to just keep going without stopping to process and release the pain of an experience will only result in it arising again and again, casting its shadow over your mind and heart, negatively affecting your relationships and disrupting you from within. It will keep you trapped in the past, unable to really thrive in the present.

We are given life to experience it, but we have to be brave. There have been times when I have gone through heartbreak so agonising that I truly wondered if I would be able to survive. Yet I always recovered eventually, and my heart could take pleasure from life again too. I learned to trust my heart. Just like yours, it has a powerful ability to go through darkness and find the light, emerging stronger and more loving than ever, again and again and again.

19.
Trusting In The Timing Of Life

IF EVERY TRAFFIC LIGHT TURNED GREEN at once there would be utter chaos! No one would end up getting anywhere! A red light is sometimes not only necessary, but a way for you to ultimately get somewhere faster. There isn't any point trying to run a red light or push ahead; though when someone is driving slowly in front of me, and I want to go fast, I can momentarily forget this.

Nonetheless, there is a scheme, a natural order of things necessary for growth to happen. Winter has to come before spring. So if you are getting a symbolic 'red light' in your life, it's okay. Some people will need to get where they are going before you. They get the green light. This may well be so they can establish connections and circumstances that will become a basis for your future steps. The sooner they get their green light, the sooner you'll get yours. So it makes sense to help each other. Someone propped at a green light is going to hold up traffic. You want to encourage people to move forward on their path, to embrace their success. It helps everyone. And when you have to wait for your turn, or someone else does, that's okay too. The universe is sort of like a celestial traffic controller, keeping the travellers out of chaos and the roads functioning so everyone can progress on their journey.

20.
Extra Credit In The School Of Life

THERE IS NO NEED TO FEEL ASHAMED if you are struggling in life. Challenges can be the universe's way of pushing you to find something incredible within that you wouldn't otherwise know existed. It could be, perhaps, your courage or fighting spirit, unconditional trust, or a heart capable of extraordinary compassion and forgiveness.

Like advanced students given a heavier workload, sometimes life dishes up extra work for those capable of growing and triumphing through a particular difficulty. It doesn't mean we can't also grow through delight and joy (thankfully!), but it does mean that disappointments, even tragedy or loss, are not a punishment or sign that we have failed. They are just opportunities to earn extra credit in the school of life.

21.

Emotional Cleansing

ENERGY AFFECTS YOU even if you don't always realise it. Thoughts, beliefs and emotions are all forms of energy. If you have ever felt caught up in the excitement of a sporting match, as though your own enthusiasm (or disappointment, depending on the way the match is going) is amplified, then you will have experienced how emotional energy from people can gather, build and cause an impact.

From the exhilaration of a New Year's Eve countdown to the mass panic of a terrorist threat discussed on the news one evening, emotional energy can be contagious. You may find yourself getting swept up in the emotional energy of groups in panic about immigration, financial fluctuations in the economy, Christmas, or even the state of your workplace during changes that have people fearing for their jobs. Or the emotional impact can be closer to home through the depression or anger of a loved one who causes you to feel drained and negative for no apparent reason.

Most of us don't think twice about physical cleansing and just assume it is necessary for good health and hygiene. It is the same for emotional and psychological hygiene. If you are taking in a lot of energy from the media (which does tend towards negativity) or from people around you, you'll need to clear it out from time to time. The easiest way to do this is to put yourself in nature, preferably near running water. If that's not practical, then grab a handful of salt – even cheap table salt will work – and jump in the bath or shower and give yourself a gentle salt scrub. If you can imagine, feel or intend that any water washing over your body is also cleansing your emotions and mind, then your physical bathing routine can easily become an emotional and psychological cleansing routine too.

22.

Sometimes Games Aren't Fun To Play

WHILST IT MAY SEEM that another person makes us feel a certain way, ultimately we are the ones who choose our responses. Someone may be grumpy, but it is our choice whether we take that on or have compassion and choose to be happy. Everyone has responsibility for their own emotional reactions – positive and negative. If you believe you are the cause of another person's mood or behaviour, or feel guilty and try to 'heal' or uplift them out of a painful experience, or believe they are the cause of yours, then you are playing emotionally manipulative games.

Why do people play such games? It is an unconscious attempt to avoid dealing with our own pain. If it is someone else's fault that we feel unhappy, we don't have to do anything about it; we tell ourselves that they are the one who has to change. Change can be hard and we may be afraid of it. In avoiding it however, we can end up making the people we care about feel dutybound to take care of our emotional needs in all sorts of unspoken ways, since we refuse to grow up emotionally and take care of ourselves.

This sort of behaviour causes long-term emotional and psychological harm to all involved. It separates us from our power, teaching us to feel frightened, insecure, doubtful, dependent and controlling. We'll become more prone to passive-aggressive behaviour and depression because we won't feel free. We'll feel we have to make the choices that suit others rather than those that are true for us. We might feel trapped, resentful and then guilty about it because we really do love the person but hate feeling responsible for their emotions.

You have the right to stop playing such games at any time, even if other players accuse you of betrayal, selfishness, not caring, being a bad person or being a big disappointment, and try to punish you with coldness, rage or rejection. If they do not want your relationship to become healthy, where you can love, nurture and care for each other, ultimately taking responsibility for your happiness and choices, you may need to step back and create some space. If the other person is unwilling or incapable of growing up emotionally, then the best choice may be to cut your ties to that person. Whatever you hope to gain by remaining in such a connection will come at too high a cost over time. There's a lot of love and goodness in the world and you deserve to experience some of that.

23.
Patience For Perfect Timing

PATIENCE IS A VIRTUE, as the expression goes. It's also a wise friend, adviser and time-saver.

There have been so many times where I have grabbed the proverbial bull by the horns and tried to wrestle a particular situation into order. Unintentionally, I have made things even more complicated and chaotic through my interference. So when I chose not to do that anymore, I noticed something else happening instead. Life would sort itself out – in ways I couldn't have imagined. I just needed to live it, not manage it. It was a relief. It was also revitalising, and freed up a lot more energy I could use to create with instead of attempting to control.

So if I get impatient, I remind myself not to worry. Life has a habit of sorting things out, in the perfect way at the perfect time, to be even better than anything I could imagine for myself.

24.
Mother Nature Is Your Spiritual Teacher

NATURE IS A LIVING WISDOM SCHOOL. She teaches us daily about the spiritual laws of life. She shows us that everything changes; she shows us that death is not an ending, but simply another phase in a larger cycle. Winter always happens before the spring. When we really absorb this lesson we can relax and live with more trust in the changes that happen in our lives.

Nature's lessons bring us inner peace. Life continues even beyond death. There's beauty and functionality in diversity – we don't all have to look or behave in the same way. Growth is part of being alive and includes the shedding of old, outdated ways as we embrace the new. When we have been thinking too much (the plague of modern, technological culture) or are worrying about problems, big or small, then spending some time in nature can become therapeutic.

From the tiniest subatomic particle to the most massive swirling galaxy, nature's laws apply. We are all spiritual students in her wisdom school, learning to relax, trust and grow in the flow of life.

25.

Saying No To Say Yes

SAYING YES TO SOMETHING often means saying no to something else.

When I was younger, I dreamed of doing many things in my life. I had enough dreams and visions of what I wanted to be to cover at least ten lifetimes! For a long time I tried to pursue everything all at once. I made some progress on a lot of paths, but not much overall on any one path. I learned something useful though: if you try to do everything at once, you'll end up getting nothing done.

It is actually going to get you further, faster, if you learn to say no – even if just for now – so you can really say yes with commitment and effort to complete something else. I thought that saying no would cut me off from life. I wanted to be open to all opportunities. I was caught up in the 'fear of missing out'. However, I was wasting huge amounts of energy and not really listening to what my heart wanted. Once I paid closer attention to my heart, I stopped trying to say yes to everything and just said yes to what really felt right, whether that made sense logically or not. Progress in my life increased dramatically as a result. I achieved and experienced more than I ever had before.

Sometimes saying no is what helps you really say yes to what matters.

26.

Think Outside The Square

YOU ARE A VERY CREATIVE PERSON, although you may not always see yourself that way. Being a creative person doesn't only mean being gifted with a paintbrush.

Creative energy is like fuel in a car. It helps us get to where we want to go, even if we don't think about it most of the time. We can use creative energy in artistic ways, such as painting, writing, making music or designing a website, but we can also use it to choose a gift for a friend, cook a meal, put together an outfit, decorate a home, plan our day, plan a holiday, find a great parking spot, or respond to another person in conversation. We tend to do many of these things without realising we are being creative.

Creative people are good at finding their way around obstacles on the path to success because they are open to possibilities. When we decide to be open to *another way*, even without knowing exactly what, just that it exists, we increase our capacity for success. It's a bit like casting a wider net for fishing. You increase your chances for getting what you want by remaining open.

Success is rarely something that happens in a straight line from A to B. It is more often like a squiggly line that runs ragged all over the place with stops and starts and unpredictable changes in direction and pace. Success requires that we get creative, thinking outside the square.

If something isn't working, don't keep doing it. Treat a failure or obstacle as a chance to come up with a different approach. When you are creative you will learn and adapt, making changes to move around obstacles rather than just give up when things get difficult. Creative people don't give up. They just look for a different way to get to where they want to go.

27.
The (Dis)Comfort Zone

WHEN WE ARE GROWING FAST, rapidly heading towards healing or success, we won't always realise it at the time. Growth happens in a discomfort zone, which is where we learn.

On the journey to healing and success, we do have to apply ourselves. Sometimes you have to make an effort when you would prefer not to; but most of all, you have to be willing not to give up. You'll need to give yourself permission to keep going, no matter what, until you get to where you want to be, even if the path seems to take you in very unexpected directions without proof of progress along the way! You may even feel like you are going backwards at times. It can feel heartbreaking! But you have the power to choose not to give up. You can choose to see those times as the winter before your springtime is due.

It is important to acknowledge the smaller successes you accomplish each day. The big successes are wonderful, such as when you realise something or someone doesn't have power over you, or the big promotion or public recognition. But the small successes – such as taking a step each day, showing up to apply yourself to whatever task you are working on, choosing to hold peace and belief in your heart rather than doubt or distrust – are just as important, perhaps even more so, because without them the bigger successes cannot happen.

These small successes add up over time. Remembering that can keep us going, even when nothing seems to be happening, which is what it is going to seem like a lot of the time! In any growth cycle, the blossoming is the bit at the end. All the other non-visible parts have to happen first. The planting of the seed, its development until it gains enough strength to send out roots – all of that happens beneath the surface. Even when there is eventually a small shoot sprouting above the surface, it might not seem like much. Yet without it, there would be no flowering later on.

There is no such thing as an overnight success, even though it might appear that way from the outside. If you are wondering about getting any closer to your dream, to your goal, to your healing, the answer is – yes, keep going. Your time will come, and it will be then that you'll blossom into your success and healing as if your soul was a beautiful flower in the garden of life.

28.

Resistance & Negative Attraction

RESISTANCE DOESN'T FREE YOU; it actually binds you to what you are trying to push away, creating a negative attraction. If you have ever tried to stop thinking about a person you didn't want to think about and failed, or wanted to feel free from a past experience but couldn't stop playing it over and over in your head, then you have experienced negative attraction. Another way to say this is: what you resist, persists.

Dropping your resistance doesn't mean you are letting someone get away with something or allowing them to treat you inappropriately. You don't give up resistance and then suddenly become a doormat. When you let go of resistance you are actually saying, "I am strong enough to face this and win!"

When you stand face to face with whatever you are fighting against, even your own feelings, you put yourself in a position of surprising power. If you don't try to push it away, you give yourself the opportunity to deal with it directly. It's like being willing to confront the monster under the bed only to find that, although you imagined the worst, there's actually nothing to fear. You show up and face it head on and it loses its power over you. So whatever you have been resisting – a fear that you aren't loveable, aren't good enough, aren't talented enough, aren't going to be okay financially, or won't find your way professionally – face it head on. Shine a torch on it just like you would under the bed to see what's there.

When we have the guts to look at our fears up close and personal and ask ourselves, "Well, do I really believe that is going to happen after all?", most of the time the answer will be, "No, not really."

Most of the things you fear are never going to happen. And if you are put in situations where you are frightened – because sometimes life can seem scary – it will only be because there is a future version of you, waiting on the other side of your fear, calling you towards a better life. Take courage in hand and walk through it.

29.

I Like You

YOU NEVER NEED TO WORRY that there isn't enough love to go around. The more you give, the more it grows. Love is a healing medicine for mind, body and soul. Feeling grumpy, despairing or depressed? Try kindness, or smile at someone. Or if you can't quite summon that, do something nice for yourself. You deserve kindness and love as much as anyone else.

Whenever you catch yourself thinking something mean about yourself or another, substitute it for a loving thought. Rather than judging, why not have the thought, *Universe, please help that person; they seem to be having a rough day!* Some people have been so deprived of encouragement they don't really know what it sounds or feels like, or are suspicious of it. You may be the same. You might think it is indulgent or false. Yet genuine encouragement – even just a positive thought about another person – may be the difference between them giving up and sinking into doubt and depression, or choosing to believe in themselves and keep going!

Someone who doesn't believe in themselves enough to take action on their dreams needs more self-love, not more criticism. This applies to you and to others. You can put this into practice by saying to yourself daily: "I like you. You're doing a great job there. I am proud of you."

Not really believing in it? Keep going. Most of the critical thoughts we believe about ourselves are utter rubbish. They have gained power through repetition. Like a well-worn pathway, it's easier to fall back to those. But if we repeat new thoughts, new internal dialogue, we'll create a new pathway. It will be a nicer one to travel on; and the more we use it, the less we'll use the old one. Eventually, the old one will be overgrown and it will actually be easier to live on the new pathway because it feels better.

Science has documented the existence of these pathways in the brain, and has also noted that they can be changed. The scientific term for this is 'neuroplasticity', the idea that the brain can be physically changed through the power of our thoughts. We lay those pathways with the thoughts we choose to have about ourselves and the world. We can choose loving, positive and beautiful thoughts to create a life path for ourselves that is loving, positive and beautiful too.

30.

Opening Doors

THE RIGHT DOOR WILL OPEN at the right time. That can mean that a person or opportunity shows up in your life, out of the blue, to help you when you need it. If life doesn't seem to be working out the way you want, then you can trust that it still will, in an even better way, but you can't see it yet. Even when something seems like a perfect idea, the reality may be that it's not so perfect for you. The timing could be off or the chemistry for success just won't be there. You don't have to understand it at the time, but you can trust that the right things will happen at the right time. What is destined and meant for you will come, and what is not, won't. With hindsight, the pain of not getting what you want exactly when you want it often turns into relief and gratitude. You realise how inferior that thing would have been compared to what you eventually received and at the perfect time you received it.

31.

Empty To Receive

WHEN YOU CREATE SPACE IN YOUR LIFE, perhaps by letting someone or something go, you create room to receive. Imagine a room containing the things you really love with enough space to really notice and enjoy them. Now compare that to a room crammed tight with so much clutter – some of which you don't even like – that you can't find anything, even a place to sit! There is so much clutter it feels like there isn't much room to breathe, let alone add anything else. It feels suffocating.

If we hold on to too much of anything we can end up feeling suffocated, panicked and trapped. We also block the universe from sending us something exciting, fresh and new. If you want to attract more into your life, create some room for it. Do a clear out, physically, emotionally, of relationships that aren't really animated anymore but going through the motions because of shared history and not much else. Clear out the belongings you don't really use, love or treasure. Give them away or sell them.

Becoming empty could trigger fear – fear that you'll not have enough if you don't hold on, fear that if you let go you'll be left alone, left with nothing. But life doesn't operate like that. I remember once seeing the aftermath of a bushfire in an Australian national park. Everything seemed charcoal black as though there was only death, emptiness, nothing left. Then I noticed a charred tree covered with fresh green leaves sprouting up so quickly! Life is irrepressible. It cannot help but want to thrive.

Letting people or possessions go is your clear broadcast to the universe asking for something new and improved to come to you. The more you release, the more open you can be to receive. And you will receive. Remember that expression 'ask and you shall receive'? Well, it's true. Just think of letting go as your way of asking, and life shall take care of the rest.

32.

The Courage To Be Different

IT TAKES COURAGE TO BE YOURSELF. You might try to hide certain things or fit in with whatever you think is normal, but in truth there is no such thing as normal. There are just many different people in this world, some of whom are up-front and proud of their uniqueness, and others who are still learning it's okay to just be themselves.

You'll need courage to embrace the things that make you different. Sometimes being yourself means you will need to believe in something or live a way other people will not necessarily respect or understand. There will be times when you may feel alone, separate from the crowd, even frightened or a bit crazy. That's okay. Keep living your life and taking your journey. If you remember not to get stuck trying to fit in and to keep travelling along your path instead, eventually, you'll find a place where you can be yourself, as different, unique and honest as you dare to be, and still feel like you belong.

There is a story about an ugly duckling. It starts with a swan egg that somehow ends up in a nest of duck eggs. The 'duckling' is born in that nest of eggs. He doesn't know he is a swan. All he knows is he doesn't fit in, and he is teased and criticised for it. His life journey takes him on a long adventure, away from the ducks, into the company of cats and geese, and even during one hard winter he is all alone. He has been judged and misunderstood and criticised his whole life. He feels miserable. Then one day, after that long, lonely winter, he sees the most beautiful birds he could ever imagine: a flock of swans. He is so captivated by how lovely they are he decides to approach them because even though he has been told, time and time again, there's something 'not right' about him, he is brave. When the swans welcome him immediately as their own he is shocked. He looks down at his reflection on the lake and sees something even more unexpected. He is one of those beautiful birds! He is a swan. He has come home.

It is said that home is where the heart is. Trust your heart, live your truth and, if you need to leave people behind on your journey, don't be afraid. Keep going. It might be a big adventure, but eventually you will find the place you belong. Your heart will lead you home.

33.
Sometimes The Quickest Way Is To Slow Down

DO YOU KNOW THE STORY of the hare and the tortoise? They are in a race. The hare scoffs at the tortoise and his slow methodical approach, and rushes ahead so quickly that eventually he tires himself out and falls asleep instead of crossing the finish line. The tortoise happily ambles on past him and wins the race.

So here we have the story that illustrates the old maxim, 'slow and steady wins the race'. Now, I heard this story as a child, but it didn't stop me from trying to rush ahead as if I could speed up my destiny through sheer strength of will! It was a joke amongst my friends as to how fast I could write a book or produce a CD; and although it's true that I create relatively quickly, focusing on speed meant that sometimes I ended up doing more than I needed to. I was fast but also inefficient! It took me a few years to work this out. Then I decided I wanted to be more effective in my life, and to do that I had to slow down – at least a little! However, I am ambitious, passionate and headstrong. Learning to take a gentler pace was a hard lesson for me. Every time I tried to push faster for something to happen, I ended up wasting time, money and energy. I came to realise it wasn't up to me to bend life to my will, but to learn to respect the wisdom and timing of life and work with it rather than throw myself against it.

Of course, in that process of tempering my extreme desire to push for a result, something great happened. I became more productive, achieving more with less struggle. I still worked hard to accomplish my tasks; but I learned to put my energy into things that would respond to it, such as my daily work, rather than to throw it away in trying to control something I could never control – the pace of life itself. I relaxed, was willing to slow down, and the manifestation of my dreams naturally quickened without me trying to force it.

34.

Meeting Your Own Expectations

YOU DON'T HAVE THE POWER TO CONTROL what people think of you. It's highly likely that in your life you will have people that absolutely love you and others that won't like you at all – possibly for the very same reasons!

If you let the opinion another has of you – for better or worse – become relevant to your sense of self-esteem and self-confidence, you'll struggle more than you need to. Other people's views are not really anything to do with you anyway. A person's opinion tells you more about their personal preferences, their particular likes and dislikes.

Opinions are as fickle as the weather. I've never seen anything quite so vicious as someone turning against a former idol when they have proved themselves to be an ordinary (though perhaps talented) human being – loved and adored one moment, and viciously criticised and despised the next! Did that former idol change dramatically in value or essence? Of course not. But opinions can change dramatically in a split second, even whilst the person in question remains just as they ever were.

I receive many messages from people around the world saying truly beautiful things about how they have connected with my work. I feel genuinely moved by these messages. Yet I know that it is up to me to respect what I do whether others appreciate it or not. When a product sells very well I don't feel as though I am a better person. I am happy because I realise it has struck a chord with people and is helping them, which is why I created it in the first place. It feels good to have that success, especially when there were so many years where I just couldn't seem to reach people at all. But it doesn't change my opinion of myself as a person. I am still as I was before anyone knew of my work.

It can be harder to deal with situations where the opinions about you are negative, particularly if the person in question is quite willing to share it with as many people as possible! In Australia, we call this the 'tall poppy syndrome'. It refers to the desire to cut others down to make yourself feel better. Considering that in Australia it is considered a real put-down to say, "You love yourself!", then this is not a surprising phenomenon. Fortunately, being Australian also teaches you to keep a sense of humour about it all, to not take yourself quite so seriously, so that even whilst you live a happy and successful life you can also keep your feet on the ground. It's amazing how this gives you a sense of just simply liking yourself and not having to prove anything to anyone, or live up (or down) to another's opinion.

35.

Let Your Feelings Lead

THE VERY BEST THINGS IN MY LIFE happen when I trust what I feel. I frequently make decisions that leave the more logically-minded of my acquaintance wondering what the hell I am doing! That's fine. I know that I am choosing intuition over logic and I prefer it that way.

As I have learned to let my intuition guide me, I have found a sense of peace and trust that eluded me when I was trying to live according to logic alone, climbing the corporate ladder, doing all the things I was supposed to do to become what other people defined as successful. The more I tried to live that way, the more miserable I felt, so eventually, I gave it up. The success I wanted to experience needed to be something that actually made me happy, fulfilled and feel like it meant something to the world. It turns out there was a part of me, deep within, beyond logic, trying to tell me that all along. It knew what I needed to be happy in my life, and how to get there.

This same inner wisdom is in you too. It communicates to us through our feelings. That path is not always an easy one. There are plenty of challenges on the journey. But it's far more enjoyable to work towards something that feels meaningful and brings satisfaction along the way.

Working hard for something that makes you miserable is not a path to success; it's just a path to feeling miserable! If we are going to put effort into something, it may as well be for something we love. If we want to live a life that is more about love and less about misery, then we are going to have to trust ourselves and let our feelings lead.

36.
All That Glitters Is Not Gold

MY MOTHER TAUGHT ME many valuable lessons as a child. One was – to use her words – all that glitters is not gold. She was trying to help me gain some wisdom when I had become entranced by a clique at school. This group of girls seemed so glamorous to me and I wanted to be just like them. So I set about infiltrating their circle, much to the chagrin of my other group of friends who felt rejected by my grass-is-greener-on-the-other-side attitude. I soon realised there was not much beyond the surface gloss of that flashy clique, and my friendships with those girls did not bring me joy.

The experience taught me what my mother knew all along: no matter how appealing an appearance, you need to look deeper to assess the true value and substance of a person or opportunity. In time, I stopped chasing the glitter, no longer feeling enchanted by it. It's sort of like losing your taste for junk food because you have found the nourishment of healthier eating more appealing – at least most of the time!

I began to recognise the gold in my life – the real, radiant and substantial connections and opportunities that brought me nourishment – and I was thankful. And this was perhaps all the more so because of my dissatisfying prior experiences with the empty appearance of glitter that didn't deliver.

37.

Disarming The Drama

IT IS POSSIBLE NOT TO GET CAUGHT UP in another person's emotional drama. You can choose to witness it without judging, without criticising, *and* without getting involved. You could think of it along the lines of the quirky Polish expression: not my circus, not my monkeys!

You can have compassion for the situation and choose not to add fuel to the fire. We might think we are supporting someone by agreeing that some person or situation is terrible and that they are right to feel outraged, or that if they want to argue with us then we have to argue back. But if such so-called support just keeps us locked in a struggle, then is it really loving? Is it really helpful?

Some people find it easy not to get embroiled in the dramas of others because they simply don't care. But if you really do care about people, it takes genuine inner strength to resist a sense of being loyal or showing support by joining in their drama. Rather than diving in and possibly drowning in suffering along with them, why not keep your feet on dry ground and throw them a line to pull themselves out instead? Sometimes you will help another person through what you choose *not* to do.

The more we learn how to stay in our centre and not get dragged into the latest drama of friends, colleagues or family, or the human collective (especially after a terrorist threat, a political upheaval or when a negative financial prediction becomes a hot topic in the media and sets off a wave of reactive panic), the more we can help to bring peace to others, which is what the world needs more of right now.

38.
The Art Of Receiving

YOU MAY BE SO FOCUSED on what you think you want that you forget to pay attention to really receiving what you are given. Being able to receive requires a generous heart. You might think there is only generosity in the giving; but if you are generous in receiving, you give something pleasurable to the giver and allow yourself to really benefit from the gift. Otherwise, it's like eating without really tasting the food and so much potential pleasure is lost.

Many of us have *so* much in our lives, yet how often do we regularly feel content with what we have? Are we really satisfied? This is a lack of nourishment that comes when you are not able to really digest what you are given. It can literally be physical – being overfed and undernourished which is very common in the Western world. It can also be an inability to really receive a compliment, a genuine offer of help or a kind and supportive comment.

If we don't know how to receive, no matter how much we 'get', we will not be filled by it. Nothing will ever feel like it's enough. To be able to receive, we have to be willing to acknowledge vulnerability – that someone has made an impact on us, that we need help or have been moved by something another person has said, done or given us. We need to have an open heart as well as open hands.

39.

Destructive Urges

THERE IS A DESTRUCTIVE STREAK IN NATURE, and in human nature too. Sometimes this is helpful, clearing away the old to make way for the new. There will always need to be winter before spring can come. But sometimes it is not so helpful. A single careless word or action could undo months' or even years' worth of hard work. With a masterstroke of sabotage we might betray the trust of a loved one and poison a cherished relationship. Or we might push away the people we want to be close to, with apparently uncontrollable outbursts of cruelty and anger.

The destructive urge within can be made to help rather than hinder us, if we are willing to acknowledge our potential to be our own worst enemy. We need to take the advice from Sun Tzu's *The Art of War*, which suggests that it is wise to keep your friends close and your enemies closer. You want to know what the potentially dangerous and destructive part of you is up to so you can head it off before it causes real damage. If you try to ignore this part of you and pretend it doesn't exist, it will steal from you. The happiness, health and effort you put into building a life for yourself will be undermined by sabotaging choices – the type of people you invite into your life will inhibit your efforts and you'll even find your behaviour undoing all the good you've tried to attain.

There is an expression in the addiction recovery movement that if you don't hug your demons they'll bite you on the backside. The destructiveness in us is one of those demons that needs hugging. That doesn't mean we give it free licence to make ourselves and our loved ones miserable by acting out our darkest impulses. It means we get to know the part of us that wants to smash that sandcastle on the beach and ask it to help us. It's sort of like turning a wild rampaging boar into a family watchdog.

You learn to use your destructive nature for positive purposes – a sort of constructive use of destruction. It helps you do a ruthless clean out of your home, or lets you know when you've just been too disciplined and need to let your hair down and have a break. It lets you know when you are feeling trapped in a relationship and need some 'me' time. If you have been too much of the 'good girl' or 'nice guy' tending to the needs of others, it pushes you to do something for yourself. It doesn't have to take over your life.

It isn't wise to become complacent about this part of you; but if you are willing to acknowledge its existence and learn to speak its language, you'll find that you can use it as a fire to keep your house warm, rather than burn the whole thing down.

40.

Choose To Be Happy

SOMETIMES WE DON'T JUST DELAY GRATIFICATION, being willing to work hard for something without getting an instant pay-off. Sometimes we delay gratitude as well. This happens when we put off celebration, a sense of happiness and contentment in life until 'later'. Usually, in our fantasy of that 'later' time, we will have changed jobs, made more money, lost weight, got a new car or bought our own home, or met our soul mate or got married, had a baby, been published, or reached any number of 'goalposts' previously in the distance.

I once went through a phase where I would put off wearing new clothes. They would sit in my wardrobe for 'later'. After several years went by and those lovely dresses still weren't worn, I started to wonder exactly what I was waiting for! I realised that at some level I was waiting for my life to happen later and was living as if now was just in the meantime and not particularly special.

Deciding to be happy with what you have now, to treat life as something to celebrate each day, will have you feeling more content and peaceful deep within. Celebrate even in small ways, such as wearing a nice piece of clothing or having gratitude for things in life going well, and maybe, if you are feeling very spiritual, by having gratitude for the challenges helping you to grow. It doesn't mean you have to give up on your goals. It just means you acknowledge living in the present moment and that you have the power to choose to enjoy that too. You can then make the delightful and freeing discovery that things don't need to be perfect for a person to choose to be happy.

41.

Alone But Not Lonely

DON'T BE AFRAID OF BEING ALONE for a time. If you are brave enough to step away from relationships when it is time to do so, you'll go through times where you are on your own. You might feel quite alone in the world, but it won't be forever and it doesn't have to be something to resist. You may even come to enjoy those times if you learn to like your own company.

In those in-between times where you are in life's transit lounge, perhaps because you've moved country or let go of a circle of friends (or been booted out due to divorce, relocation or being fired from your job) you'll relax because you won't be in fear of being alone for a while. Loneliness can be a part of life. It's not constant and it's okay to feel it sometimes.

The loneliest I have ever felt was whilst I was in a committed relationship with a man that I truly loved, but who couldn't really relate to me or receive me. I never again confused company of others with connection. Sometimes those two things go together, sometimes not. I also realised that solitude and loneliness don't always go together either. My feelings of great affection and connection with the world can sometimes happen when I am on my own, sitting quietly in contemplation, just falling in love with humanity. Being in solitude for a time is also a chance to feel your own feelings and find your own truths. And then when you are back in a relationship again, because you will be eventually, it is all the more authentic and nourishing.

42.

Progress Is Non-Linear

WHEN YOU ARE MAKING PROGRESS towards living a dream or healing an issue, you won't necessarily feel like you are making progress. Progress has its own trajectory and it's curvier than my hips!

The path to success meanders all over the place. Straight lines are for geometry lessons. Life is made up of kinks and curves, bends and detours. To journey along the winding road to success, we need flexibility of mind. You don't have to give up on your dream, but you will need to let go of how you think you are going to get there again and again.

You can compare this to driving a car down a straight road. You don't just hold the wheel in one position. There are many micro adjustments needed to keep moving ahead. So it is with travelling along our life path. We have to be willing to 'be adjusted' by life, so that we stay true to our course.

43.

Bless This Rest

REST IS IMPORTANT. Lizards can teach us something about this. They lie about, apparently not doing much, yet when they need to move they are incredibly swift. One minute they are in repose, the next they are suddenly out of sight! The lizard has grace and speed when needed because it conserves energy through resting at other times.

Whenever life is telling me something big is coming, and I need to be ready to take advantage of it, a lizard shows up. Mother Nature keeps sending them my way until I get the message. Living in Australia most of the time, that means the types of lizards I will see can be rather large. So if I don't take the hint with one of the many smaller lizards in the back garden, I can end up locking eyes with a big goanna in the front yard! That certainly makes me pay attention.

The lizard is also a sign that much can be happening in the bigger scheme of things, even if there apparently is not much going on at that moment for you. All that lizardly lolling about can be essential 'productive downtime' making you capable of running with the more active moments about to suddenly happen.

Sometimes you need to sprint, to paddle like a surfer, to catch that spectacular, once-in-a-lifetime wave of an opportunity. If you are overwhelmed, overloaded and can't even summon enough energy to attend to what is already happening, you'll lack the energy you need to catch the wave.

So take some time lying in the sun in your garden or some other version of restful lizard-wisdom. Then you'll be ready to move, quick as lightning, when the time is right.

44.
Let Go To Receive

DETACHMENT AND LETTING GO are essential to receive. It might seem back to front, but if you've ever been with someone who has clung to you so tightly you felt suffocated and wanted to escape as quickly as possible, then you'll understand how holding on can have the effect of pushing away!

Letting go doesn't mean no longer caring or giving up on something. It is actually what is necessary to get the ball rolling on any project or vision you want to create. If you want to throw a ball through the air you have to let go. Letting go sets things in motion.

45.
Climbing The Right Mountain

OVER THE YEARS I have chased many ambitious goals. I climbed the requisite mountains for those goals to be obtained; and despite the outward appearance of success, inside I was very unhappy. I conceded that perhaps I didn't know all there was to know about what could make me happy!

I decided to try an experiment. I knew what I wanted from my life – to feel fulfilled and loved and to offer something to the world that would help as many people as possible. I wanted to do that creatively and enjoy the process as much as possible. I wanted to become the best version of myself that I possibly could. I believed that life wanted that for me too. So I decided to stop trying to control how all that happened (to be blunt, my attempts hadn't worked out so well) and to take a chance on trusting in life to guide me. Life provided what was needed for many creatures to thrive. Why should I not be one of them?

So I learned to feel and follow my inner guiding senses, rather than think and drive my path forward by my own hand. The transition was hard. I felt crazy sometimes, as my internal guide nudged me to take risks and make choices I didn't always understand and rarely felt comfortable taking. I didn't want to go back to making myself miserable chasing so-called success in the way I once had; so I trusted those inner nudges more than I doubted, and acted on them.

Over time, it became second nature to listen to my dreams and intuitions, instincts and feelings, and I used those as the basis for my life choices. What started out as awkward eventually became a sense of loving, helpful, protective guidance that I trusted completely and couldn't imagine living without! Sometimes I would even feel a knowing about a situation and how to deal with it in advance, so that when the time for challenge came I knew how to respond. When I needed information, it came to me in a timely fashion. But that doesn't mean I was suddenly back in control again. I usually had no clue where I was being led. Nonetheless, I experienced successes that enhanced my happiness instead of depleting it.

I understand that sometimes we need to prove that we can accomplish what we set out to do; that's a part of our maturing process. Eventually though, we'll realise that of course we can accomplish many things if we set our minds to it but then perhaps be ready to give up directing the course of our lives and trust in the guiding hand of life instead. Then the mountains we climb will be the right mountains.

46.

Choose The Company You Keep

THE PEOPLE YOU HAVE IN YOUR LIFE can become your greatest liability or your greatest asset. Respectful relationships can help you keep faith in yourself and bring out the best in you. Disrespectful ones – even if there is a claim to love within that relationship – will slowly erode your sense of who you are; and, if left unchecked, can eat away at your dignity and self-regard until you forget who you are and begin a spiralling descent into selfdoubt and even self-hatred.

The right people in your life will be able to give and receive. When you have conflict in healthy relationships, all parties will look for a solution that helps the relationship, rather than to try to make one person right, the winner, at the expense of the other.

The wrong people for you, even if they seem to be offering the right opportunity, will take from you without thought. You could get angry about it, but it's better to just become wise. A shark will typically behave like a shark. Being nice to the shark isn't going to stop it from biting you. It's better to trust your intuition in the first place and save yourself the pain of a shark bite later on. Sometimes this means you'll have to let an opportunity go or otherwise be disappointed because you wanted that someone to be more loving or kind.

People will show you who they are almost immediately. We only make painful choices when we ignore the signs – what they say and what they do – that would otherwise set off alarm bells in our intuition. We often do that because we don't want to give up our fantasy of how we imagine things could work out. That sort of behaviour is very naive and will bring you pain.

You'll find it's worth walking away from the wrong people, so you'll have room in your heart, and your life, for the right ones.

47.
Sacred Warrior

THERE'S A WAY TO FIGHT that doesn't involve violence or sinking to the level of your attacker. It can be all too tempting to fight fire with fire, but there's a saying that you shouldn't get down and roll around in the mud with a pig because the pig enjoys it. If your way is of the heart, or is less enthusiastic about slinging mud, then you'll need to be more strategic in your method of warfare. I think of it as the way of the sacred warrior, the one who fights with integrity and strength.

Fear is the cause of anger and aggression. If someone is threatened or afraid of you, perhaps because you speak a truth they are not ready for yet, then they need your compassion – but not your indulgence. You can have compassion for another and still firmly define your boundaries and choose what sort of behaviour you are willing to accept in your relationships.

If someone is emotionally immature, they will tend to use relationships as emotional dumping grounds – for their bad moods, their fears, their doubts. They will pick a fight to off-load their stuff, leaving you feeling awful and them feeling better once it is over. This is not okay. It is wise to refuse to play such an unhealthy game with someone. More often than not, when you refuse to sling mud, those who like to fight that way will move on to find someone else who will. It can be sad to lose someone you love, but life is too short to invest your time and energy into those who happily take from you and give nothing in return. As the expression goes, don't cross an ocean for a person who wouldn't jump a puddle for you. Have compassion, but know your worth. Treat yourself with respect, even if that means taking a stand or moving on to where it may seem easier to just toe the line.

Once a battle starts with your self-respect there will always come a time where you'll have had enough and have to assert yourself. It's just a question of when. And such a battle is best nipped in the bud as soon as possible, before it becomes an all-out war. As my grandfather used to say about my grandmother, "You can put your heel on her, but watch out if you try to grind it in!"

48.
Emotional Genius

YOUR EMOTIONS CAN BECOME YOUR BEST FRIEND, part of an internal guidance system capable of uncensored honesty in a way your mind could never be. They never ever have to make sense logically in order to be valuable and accurate. Emotions don't have to be logical because they are intuitive and instinctive. Therein lies their value. Emotions operate outside of the limitations of the logical mind. If you are frightened of what you don't immediately understand (as many people are) then you'll need to learn to have some trust and curiosity as you explore the intuitive language of your emotions.

When I started exploring my emotional life in therapy, after having been stuck in my head throughout years of studying law at university, my emotional intelligence was at an all-time low. I was intuitive enough to understand that I needed to get out of my head and tap into my emotions if I wanted to heal my depression and near-constant sense of anxiety, as well as find my way out of a legal career and into something I actually *wanted* to do with my life. Yet I wasn't comfortable in the unpredictable and constantly changing world of my emotions. I used to live in my head to try and avoid chaos and unpredictability; yet, diving into my emotions felt like I was in an ocean where there was only constant change! I had no idea how to keep up with it all.

Eventually, I learned that I didn't have to understand or analyse everything I felt, but could trust that my emotions would give me valuable messages when I needed them. I found that if I didn't get the message straight away, the emotion would simply keep coming up again and again until I did. So if I felt inexplicably angry with someone, it was likely that they were either trying to take advantage of me or crossing a boundary that I couldn't consciously articulate. If I felt fear it meant I was either growing (and therefore outside my comfort zone) or something untoward was going on and I needed, as quickly as possible, to get away from whatever toxic person, place or thing I was unwittingly being drawn towards. I realised that when my mind wasn't questioning the validity of my feelings, trying to rationalise them, my emotions would give me valuable insights into people and their agendas.

The more I learned to trust these insights, the quicker I could sort out issues, often before they developed to the point where it would be extremely painful and complicated. It's worthwhile learning to swim in your emotional waters rather than remaining in your head for fear of drowning. There is just too much value in them and too much pain if you try to ignore them for too long. Besides, once you get the hang of swimming, it can even be quite fun.

49.

Choose Your Beliefs

BELIEFS CAN CHANGE OVER TIME. We may outgrow a belief when we have enough life experience to challenge it. This can then cause us to believe in something else instead. But we don't have to wait for life to push us to change; we can take the initiative and change our beliefs because we want to become happier or more at peace with a situation.

When you change what you believe about a situation, the situation itself will change. To change a belief, start by asking yourself what you believe in! Most of the time we are driven by beliefs we are not aware of consciously. You'll need to really think what it is you believe about money, work, love, religion, happiness, life, health and relationships.

If you find it helpful, you can write a list of those beliefs. They may seem obvious and true to you. You could even call the list 'The things I think I know about … (love or money, or whatever issue you are working on)'. The next step is to question every one of those beliefs (unless you feel they are making you happy and healthy in life).

You can confront any belief with the following questions. Is this the only possible way to feel about this issue? What could be a way to think about this that would make me feel the happiest?

Then you write another list if you wish, a list of upgraded beliefs. You might think that this is a 'wishful thinking' list, but beliefs are wishes (positive or negative) we have given ourselves permission to treat as truths. You can do that with thoughts that make you feel happy, optimistic and empowered just as much as you can with thoughts that make you feel sad, pessimistic and frightened.

This process of questioning will probably make you, and those close to you, uncomfortable for a while. Change can bring up insecurities. Your loved ones might wonder, if you change a lot, whether you will still love them and have room for them in your life. You may wonder the same thing about them! But choosing to change your beliefs, to change your life for the better, makes you a happier person capable of more love, not less.

50.

Love Sometimes Means Letting Go

BEING HUMAN means at some point you will experience loss. I have loved and lost many times. I have deeply cherished the people and pets I have lost. When it was time to let go – sometimes through a relationship break-up, sometimes through death – the pain of loss felt as though it tore me apart. My body endured a painful grieving process. No matter how many times you go through that it never seems to get any easier.

In the face of loss, human beings often feel shock, denial, anger and horror at its abruptness (especially death, even if you've had time to prepare yourself mentally when someone has been unwell for a long time). Even if you have wanted to leave a relationship, or were happy your loved one was finally free from suffering, you will still need to grieve. Every time I go through grief, I wonder the same things. *Will it ever end? Will life ever feel normal or happy again?* The answer to both questions is yes, eventually.

When my beloved pet died, an adopted cat who had lived with me for nearly twelve years, I was overcome with grief. To help myself deal with the loss, I created a small shrine and placed a picture of my beautiful cat there. As well as a candle, I also placed there a picture of a holy man from India I prayed to, and asked him to look out for my cat's spirit so his passing from the earthly world into the spiritual world was safe and loving.

For three days following my cat's passing, I kept the candle burning (carefully!) day and night. During that time I dreamed of my lovely cat several times, and after a day or so I felt a sense of deep peace rather than anxiety or despair when I thought about him. I knew this was my 'sign' that he was okay. He had crossed over and was happy and safe.

Beneath even my most painful moments of heartache, there was something unexpectedly comforting in the realisation that whilst his journey couldn't continue on the earth with me, his spirit lived on. I missed the furry, fluffy reality of his body, but what I wanted more than anything was to know that he was all right without me there to look after him. There was something so kind and reassuring in this experience to know that, in death, although we feel the pain of loss, the spirit in question is not lost at all, is not in pain, is not alone, and is received lovingly into an embracing spiritual world that cares for it and loves it without question.

51.

What We Are Taught To Believe

MUCH OF THE TIME we confuse what we believe with what is true, especially inherited beliefs from family, religion or culture. Many people believing in something might make that belief seem more familiar or powerful, but it doesn't make it any more true. We might believe that to be happy we have to be married, get a promotion or win the lottery. The belief will make us act like it is true, but if we were to change the belief then we would be free to act as if something else were true instead. If you changed your belief – say, you could choose to be happy anytime you wished, no matter what was happening – then the ways you could be happy would increase and your life would improve. Some beliefs will work well for us, supporting us in living well.

As a child I was taught that a woman could be strong and independent, and that uniqueness and not fitting in could be beautiful. Those beliefs work well for me and I have held on to them. However, some beliefs can be like a strangling vice around our necks, forcing us to behave in ways that lead us down the path to misery. A belief may be widely held as truth, but that has no bearing upon whether or not it is going to help us live a better life. We need some healthy disregard for authority if we are going to confront family rules, or social beliefs about age, gender or religion, or expectations based on our level of education, or our social or financial status. It doesn't mean you are suddenly going to become a harmful and destructive force in society. You can still respect another person's right to believe in whatever they choose, just as you have that right too.

Once you start changing beliefs and see how it improves your life, you'll want more of it. It can feel rebellious in the best and most liberating sense of the word. Perhaps you are ready for this sort of freedom, to challenge what you've been taught to believe, to choose to create a new reality for yourself. If so, let the rebel within you get to it!

52.
Comparison Isn't Helpful

AS TEMPTING AS IT CAN BE to compare yourself to others, it isn't very helpful. People sometimes say they compete with another to bring out the best in themselves, but I question whether that is truthful. Being inspired by someone brings out the best in you. Competing isn't about becoming a better you, it's about becoming better than someone else. The truth of how we are going in life, from a spiritual perspective, is not about where we appear to be doing better compared to someone else, but how much we are growing within.

Advanced souls often come into this world with challenges to face, bigger challenges than a younger soul would be able to handle. It is assumed that the advanced soul will be able to go far in life, so they start off further back in the field with more obstacles in their way, perhaps so they don't find life too easy! So for an advanced soul, life will often contain some darkly challenging experiences, typically (but not only), early on in life. That could include death, divorce, depression, abuse or addiction. These challenges give your spiritual light a chance to fight and grow stronger, rather than lying about on the lounge of life, not really doing anything. Spiritually speaking, having an easier life is not a sign that you are spiritually advanced. Being able to transform challenges into wisdom, compassion and a willingness to feel happiness or joy whenever you can – well, *those* are the signs that you are doing well in life at a spiritual level. If you have a lot of good things in your life – including perhaps money and talent – then spiritually, you're responsible for giving more to help others in the world. You're responsible because you are powerful enough to do it.

If you feel you are struggling in life, it doesn't mean you aren't as successful as someone who appears to have it all sorted out. It just means you are powerful enough to grow through challenge. That doesn't mean the struggle has to last forever; it won't. It does mean you have to give yourself the benefit of the doubt. Assume that you are doing well on your life journey. If you have hit a rough spot, you are going through a spiritual test. You'll know when you've passed that test with flying colours when you have learned something useful from it, something that makes you wiser. The only thing worth comparing yourself to is where you have been compared to where you are now. Do that now. Do it again in two years, in five years, and so on. Then you'll acknowledge your growth, and feel proud and confident enough to keep on going and grow spiritually.

53.

Sometimes You Won't Know

DON'T BE SCARED OF NOT KNOWING. Zen monks sit in meditation for decades to master that one, and I can understand how it could take so long. The unknown can seem like a terrifying thing!

I once had a friend who had the admirable tendency to always be curious about unknown adventures which, in the face of my near-constant anxiety at the time, seemed rather preferable to me. Eventually, I learned to soothe myself and take on some of her adventurous attitude. I began to nurture a different belief. The unknown wasn't filled with something to be afraid of; instead, I began to see it as the bringer of unexpected blessings.

54.

The Call To Adventure

WHEN YOU ARE READY (which is not always when you think you are), life will call you to an adventure. Typically, this will mean that something goes wrong and you will have to find a way through without feeling at all equipped for the task! The more stuff that will seem to go wrong, the more you will be called to adventure.

Adventure is meant to change you from the inside. It makes you realise that you have wings. You would never know that unless you were pushed from the edge and had to at least try to fly! Adventure is not always comfortable, but when life starts happening and things seem to be chaotic and out of control, you'll know you are truly on it. And there is a reason for it: you are being pushed to find something within you didn't know was there – something good, something powerful, something helpful, something wise. So as uncomfortable as it is, you need to trust in the process.

There are certain river currents that, once you get caught in them, will pull you right down to the bed of the river. If you struggle against the current, which will be stronger than you, you'll start to drown. What you won't realise at the time is that if you let go, the river current will actually not only pull you straight down to the riverbed, but push you swiftly back up the other side. Maybe you won't want to run the risk of trusting though, and you'll struggle until you are so exhausted you will just give up. And then, instead of disaster, the very thing you will have been fighting against will be the thing that moves you to safety and new life.

It might sound rather dramatic, but if you're on one of life's adventure trails, you'll know this can be exactly what it feels like – life and death. If you don't trust, you'll struggle longer and wear yourself out. The wisdom comes from knowing when you need to fight in order to grow, and when you need to let go. If you are fighting to keep things the same, you'll not be fighting for growth. So in such cases, let go. Let what is happening in your life move you, and you'll pop up at the other side of it far more quickly and without the added discomfort of water up your nose.

55.

Passion

YOUR DREAMS AREN'T A DISTRACTION from 'real life'. If you are willing to act on them, they actually become the foundation of your future. What you dream of and yearn for will have love in it. There is no greater motivation to work hard and never give up than passion. You might think it is fear, but fear wears you out. It leaves you exhausted and once you have enough to assuage the fear, the motivation is over. You'll never grow beyond it. Passion will give you energy, keep you excited and when you are tired, it will remind you why you are working so hard. It will give you the motivation to keep going until you manifest your dreams.

If you have learned that your dreams are something you should focus on only after all the 'grown up' stuff is completed, or that they are silly compared to 'the real world', then you may not understand how important your dreams are. If so, you may not make any effort to find, explore and express your passion in the world. Perhaps you worry that you don't really have a passion when everyone else does. You just need to look for it. Your passion could be people, beauty, inspiration, family, love, education, spirituality, technology, innovation, gardening, working with animals or children, healing, business, the stock market, or health and wellbeing. Passion doesn't have to fit into a job, though for some people it will and that's great.

Whether your passion is expressed in your work or your family life, in your hobbies or volunteering efforts, or just in how you choose to live each day, deciding to make passion a priority in your life will light you up on the inside. It will give you energy and attract opportunities and people to you. If you are only just starting to listen to your heart, you may find it strange to give so much value to what you feel to your passions and your dreams. You might shoot down all sorts of wonderful ideas as impractical, foolish and unobtainable before you even give them a chance to manifest.

To let your passion come to life in the world, you have to be bold. You can't take failure personally; you just need to look at it as the universe's way of telling you to try again in a different way for a better result. The more passionate you are about something, the more you will be willing to give up the things that hold you back in life – always needing to be right, to appear perfect, to be in control or to understand what is happening. You will also be more willing to do the things that can get you far in life – to work hard, to take risks, to be different and to never give up. Your dreams aren't an indulgence to squeeze into fifteen minutes at the end of your day when you relax on the lounge and fantasise about a better life. They are telling you what you feel passionate about, what will bring the zing into your step and the light into your life.

About the Author

ALANA FAIRCHILD may not have met you yet, but she knows you. She knows that inside you is a beautiful, wise and strong being. She wants you to remember that, to trust yourself, and live a life you love, from the inside and on the outside too. If you want to find out more about Alana and her work, join her online:
www.alanafairchild.com

For more information on this
or any Blue Angel Publishing release,
please visit our website at:

www.blueangelonline.com